The author would like to thank those family members, friends and colleagues who have given their encouragement and support for this project.

A special thanks goes to Roberto Gonzalez roberto@rogolart.com | www.rogolart.ca for his wonderful creativity and expertise in illustrating and formatting this book.

The Caterpillar That Learned to Fly

Text copyright © 2015 by Sharon Clark
Illustrations copyright © 2015 by Roberto Gonzalez
All rights reserved. No part of this book may be reproduced in any form or by electronic or mechanical means – except for brief quotations for use in articles or reviews - without permission in writing from the publisher.

For information about permission to reproduce selections from this book, contact Sharon Clark at sharon.clark@me.com

Printed in the USA

ISBN: 978-0995230347 | 2nd Edition | Paperback

ISBN: 978-0995230354 | Hardcover

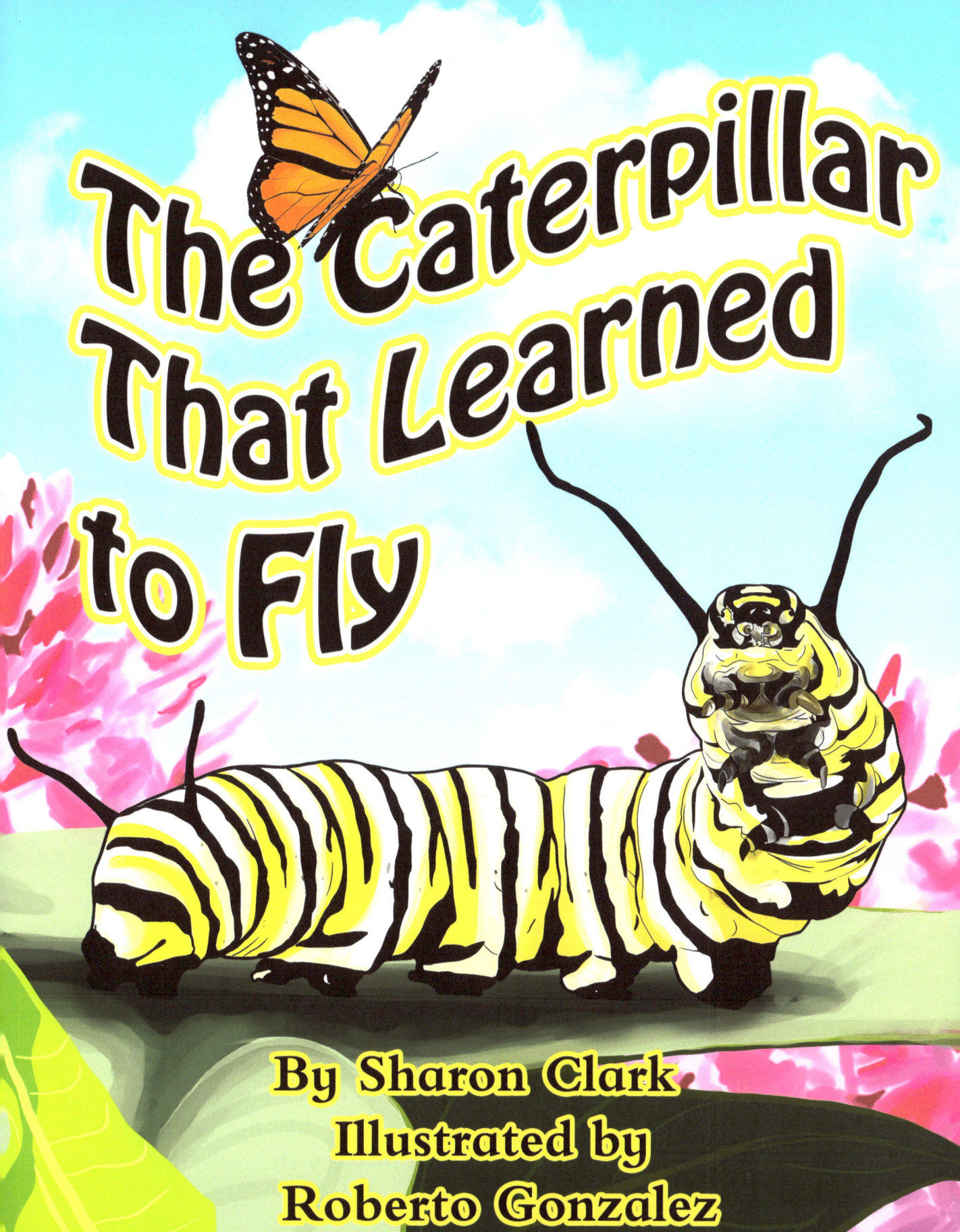

The purple flowers looked so beautiful inside the dark green milkweed leaves. They swayed slightly under the heat of the late August sun. Yet this lovely scene hid from view the activities of a creature just as wonderful to watch.

Munch, munch, munch, munch. Cutter the caterpillar had eaten his way out of his egg earlier that morning. The egg was tasty and contained many nutrients, so he had eaten every last piece. That had satisfied him for a while, but now he was getting hungry again. He found himself on the underside of a milkweed leaf where he began sampling its tiny hairs. This was pretty good too! Munch, munch, munch, munch. Finally, after a very long while he felt full, so he rested contentedly.

Before long, he became curious about his surroundings. Slowly he moved his shiny, black head from side to side. He had three pairs of true legs and five pairs of temporary legs. Now, he lifted his first pair of true legs. Cutter stretched the front of his tiny worm-like body then pulled in his back end. By doing this, he could slowly inch his body ahead. He really didn't know where he was going. Finally, after crawling ever so slowly, he reached the edge of the leaf. Unsure of what to do next, he paused. Then, he curled his smooth gray body upward to peer at the other side.

The bright sunlight startled him. Until now, he had only lived in shadow. His six pairs of simple eyes were not able to see objects, but they did detect light, darkness and movement. So, when another leaf moved slightly in the gentle breeze, its motion alarmed Cutter. As quickly as he was able, he retreated to the underside of the leaf where he felt safe from danger. Once Cutter was back in familiar surroundings, his hunger returned. Munch, munch, munch, munch. After eating all the leaf hairs around him, he began nibbling at the leaf itself. Soon, a tiny hole appeared in the leaf, which he gradually made bigger. When he had eaten until he was full, he again rested. For the remainder of his first day, Cutter continued to eat, then rest, eat, and rest again.

By morning, he had grown much bigger than the previous day. His larger body needed even more food. So again he ate. But his extra size was also preventing him from moving as easily as before. His outer skin felt tight. He found that crawling required much more effort. Afterwards, he became exhausted and he needed longer rests. The next day, Cutter had grown even more and he noticed that he could barely move. The time had come for him to shed his old, tight outer skin and make a new one. He slowly made his way to a sheltered spot under the leaf. At first, he rested quietly while his body made a new skin under the old one. Then, when the time was right, Cutter began to swallow air, which created pressure on the outer skin. Before long, the old skin split open. Then Cutter emerged with a new larger skin.

This was much better. He could move easily once more. But getting rid of the old skin used up much of Cutter's energy and he was hungry yet again. Munch, munch, munch, munch. Cutter ate the old skin that he had shed, then more milkweed leaves. He ate and rested for another two days, growing even larger.

He shed his outer skin a second time and now looked very different. His shiny black head and gray body were gone. Instead, he had a patterned skin of black, white and yellow stripes. He also now had two pairs of black tentacles. One pair was at the front of his body and one pair at the rear. These helped him feel everything around him.

He continued to eat. Now his larger size allowed him to stretch his body from one milkweed leaf to the next. Most of the time, he stayed on the underside of the leaf where his new colors blended nicely. Now, however, he was resting on the outside of a leaf. He wanted to let the rays of the bright sun warm his body.

Suddenly, a huge shadow passed overhead. Cutter felt the air above him move. His little heart began to pound. He sensed that he was in danger. Something seemed to be swooping down on him. He could not crawl away fast enough to hide. So he curled up into a tiny ball and fell from the plant. For a slow-moving creature like Cutter, this was a useful way to escape from danger quickly.

A blue jay had begun to dive towards Cutter. It had planned to eat him. However, the jay had quickly changed its mind when it saw Cutter's yellow, black and white stripes. When it had eaten a caterpillar like this before, it had become sick afterwards. The milkweed plant, on which Cutter fed, contains chemicals that are not harmful to caterpillars. But these chemicals are poisonous to many animals that eat the caterpillars. So this blue jay remembered its previous unpleasant experience and decided to find a meal elsewhere.

But now Cutter was on the ground. All he wanted to do was return to familiar surroundings. Yet, he couldn't see well enough to tell where the milkweed plants were. And he was getting very hungry. Whatever would he do? Cutter began exploring this new environment, lifting one pair of legs, then another. Grass stalks were everywhere. This made moving forward difficult. All he could do was slowly inch his way around them. He had no idea where he was going, but he crawled on anyway. Cutter hoped that he would find some milkweed plants soon because he was getting so-o-o hungry.

Eventually, he did find what he was searching for. He was lucky that his mother had carefully selected his nesting site. She had laid his egg on a milkweed plant that was among many others. If she hadn't done that, he might easily have died of starvation. So, when Cutter discovered another milkweed plant, he grabbed onto its stalk with his specialized hooks on his temporary legs. Slowly he began climbing upward, nibbling as he went..

As the days and weeks passed, Cutter continued to get bigger. He shed his outer skin two more times. One day, he began to feel strangely different. Though his outer skin again felt tight, he also felt very tired. He sensed that he needed a long rest, much longer than he'd ever had before. With a sense of urgency, he began searching for a protected spot. Finally, he found a branch on the plant's stalk that was surrounded by many leaves. It would shelter Cutter not only from the wind and rain, but also from enemies. Here was where he would stay.

Soon Cutter was using his silk-making gland on his lower lip to spin a silk button onto the stalk. He then wriggled his behind into the silk button, and his specialized claspers gripped and held on. Cutter then slowly lowered his body until he was hanging upside down. He became very quiet and still.

For one last time, his outer skin began to harden. Now, however, a new skin did not form underneath. Instead, as his fifth and last skin was shed, a specialized casing formed in its place. This casing, a chrysalis, was beautiful! At first, it had blue and yellow stripes, but as it hardened it turned green. Then beautiful golden spots appeared.

Inside the chrysalis, many changes were occurring. Much of Cutter's old body was disappearing. Most of his parts were turning to liquid. But he was in a deep sleep-like state, so he felt nothing. Gradually, something wonderful was happening. A new body was being formed inside this chrysalis. This body was very different from the worm-like form that Cutter had been. By the end of one week, the chrysalis had become very clear. A new form could be seen right through it. Something black and orange, with white dots was wriggling inside the chrysalis.

Eventually the chrysalis began to twitch. The movements were slight at first. Gradually they became more noticeable. Soon the chrysalis was jerking wildly. Slight cracks began to appear on its surface. As the cracks became larger, they began to join together. Then, suddenly, a section within one of the cracks split outward. It began to curl back on itself, revealing part of the wriggling body inside. The body appeared to be struggling. As its movements became stronger, the chrysalis suddenly split open completely and a lovely creature emerged.

Cutter had turned into Flutter, a beautiful Monarch Butterfly. As Flutter clung to the outside of the chrysalis to rest, he sensed that he had changed. The five pairs of temporary legs with specialized hooks were gone. He still had the three pairs of true legs, but they were not short and stubby as before. The first pair was short and slender. They could barely be seen because Flutter held them tightly to his body.

Flutter outstretched one leg of the remaining two pairs and noticed that it was very long and slender. He suddenly realized that for some reason, he could see them very clearly. He could also see his surroundings in beautiful colors. Flutter didn't realize that his eyes were also different. He still had simple eyes for detecting light from dark. But he now also had a large pair of compound eyes that allowed him to distinguish shape and color. He could even see parts of light that were invisible to humans. He stared for an incredibly long time at the beautiful green within the milkweed leaf.

Flutter's body had also changed. His worm-like form was gone, and in its place was a short slender body. Right now his abdomen was quite swollen, as it was filled with fluid. Parts of him were wet and hanging limply downward. Flutter didn't realize that these were two beautiful wings. They were a bright orange with black stripes and white dots. This pretty pattern warned enemies not to try to eat a Monarch Butterfly just as the caterpillar striping had scared off the blue jay. The fluid from Flutter's abdomen was slowly being pumped into these wings. They began to expand and stiffen.

The warm sun was also drying them and making them capable of flight. Flutter moved them up and down slightly at first, curious as to what their function was. When he began to move them with greater force, he suddenly found himself airborne! How excited he was to have such freedom of motion! As he experimented, he realized that he could go higher or lower, faster or slower, and he could also change direction. Oh, how different his life had become!

Flutter wasted no time. Previously, he had lived only on milkweed plants. Now he had the chance to visit new places and see many new things. He set off in a westerly direction, and before long realized that something else had changed. He now had antennae that were very sensitive to smells. He picked up a wonderful scent that he quickly followed to its source. A field of wild flowers appeared before him. Flutter landed on a beautiful purple flower with a soft yellow inner centre. Suddenly, he realized that special sensors in his feet could taste this plant. It was sweet and delicious. Then his antennae picked up an even sweeter scent. His eyes could see an invisible light surrounding its source. Quickly, he uncoiled a long drinking part. He began sucking nectar as if he were drinking from a straw. His chewing mouthparts were gone. His diet of milkweed leaves was also gone. The nectar was delicious and he moved from flower to flower to drink it.

When he was full, he flew off again to explore his new world. Over hills and fields he went, taking in all the sights, smells and colors. In his previous life, he had never guessed that such a wondrous world existed. A few weeks later, the days and nights began to get cooler. Fall was approaching. Flutter had a strong desire to travel further. He found himself flying great distances southward. He didn't know where he was going. Soon, he met up with other Monarchs like himself who were headed in the same direction. Flutter saw many new things in his travels. He crossed rivers and streams. He flew over cities, highways, fields, trees and hills. He joined groups of Monarchs and flew with them. Though he was unsure of where he was going, something inside him urged him on. The Monarchs flew thousands of miles.

Finally they reached their destination. They had come to a high mountainous forest in Mexico. Flutter and his companions were joined by thousands of others like them. They would spend the winter there, clustered together on the fir trees

In the spring, they would begin to travel north again. Each butterfly would head in the direction of its birth. But they would not make it all the way back. Instead, they would have young of their own - caterpillars just like Cutter, who would turn into Monarch Butterflies. These butterflies would not live as long as Flutter, but would also have young that eventually would travel to where their ancestors were born.

About the author

Sharon Clark works in Research and has always loved science and nature. She hoped her children would develop an interest in and an appreciation for these topics, too. But when she tried to introduce her kids to such books, she was disappointed to hear them exclaim "boring mom!".

What a shame! There is wonder in discovering the intricacies of nature. We live in an amazing world. So she set out to develop a series of science and nature books that would make learning these topics fun.

Her first picture book, "9X Fun" teaches kids a fun way to learn the 9X table. Roberto Gonzalez created a cute little mouse and beautiful illustrations for this book. Now Sharon has three nature picture books, "The Honeybee That Learned to Dance", "A Strange Guest in an Ant's Nest" and this book "The Caterpillar That Learned to Fly" that all show something wondrous about what these creatures do. Roberto Gonzalez has made these books especially appealing with his superb illustrations.

Sharon hopes that parents, teachers, librarians but mostly children enjoy and learn something new from these books.

About the Illustrator

Roberto Gonzalez Lara is a Mexican-Canadian illustrator and graphic designer.
He has created all kinds of illustrations for clients all over the world.
His passion is children's book illustration. Active member of the SCBWI (Society of Children's Book Writers and Illustrators). To contact him or see more of his work, go to www.rogolart.com.

Follow Roberto on social media:

Facebook:www.facebook.com/rogolart

Freelanced: www.freelanced.com/rogola.